JOIN THE JAM

CONTENTS

Transcribed by Jeff Jacobson

Cherry Lane Music Company
Director of Publications/Project Editor: Mark Phillips
Project Coordinator: Rebecca Skidmore

ISBN 978-1-60378-287-6

Visit our website at www.cherrylaneprint.com

THE 52 SHUFFLE
(Key of E)

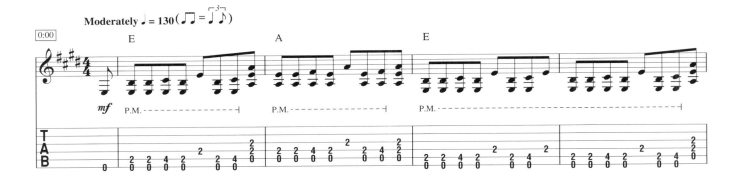

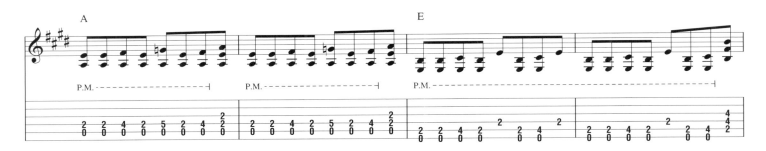

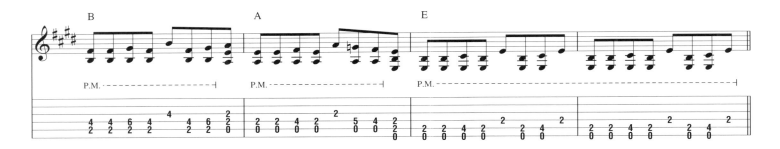

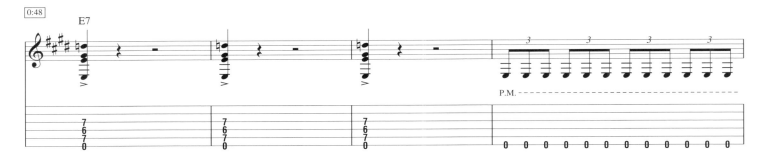

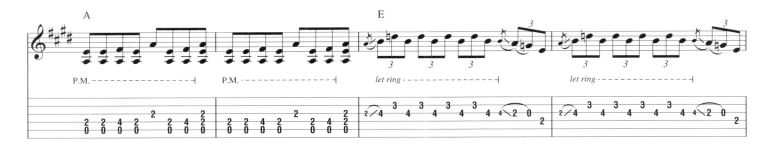

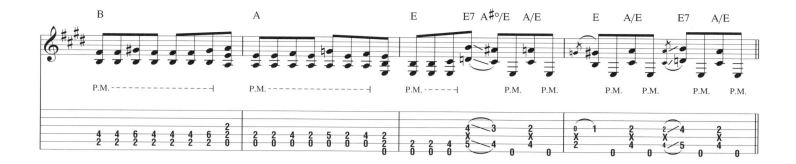

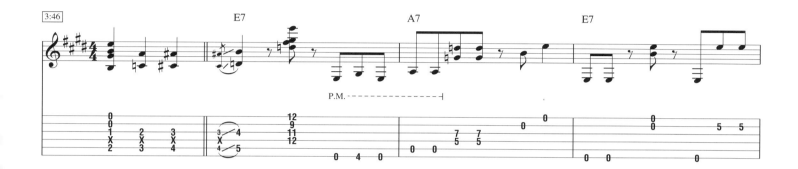

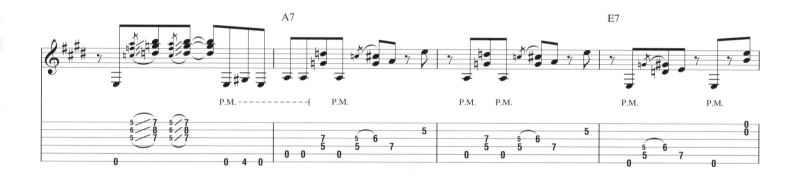

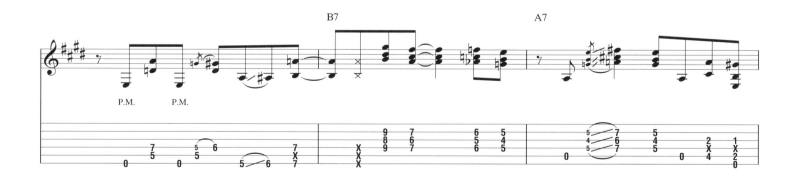

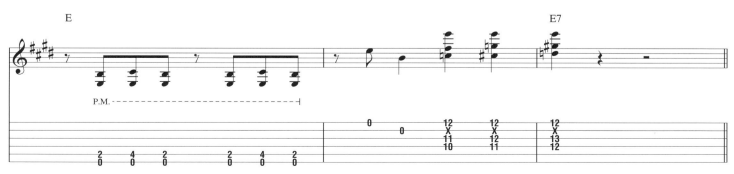

3

SLOW BLUE
(Key of C)

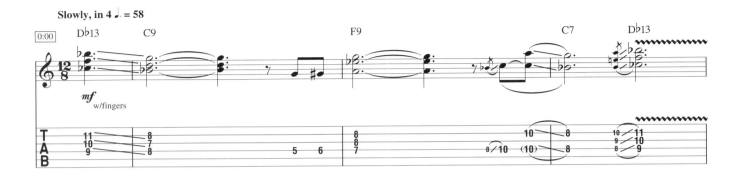

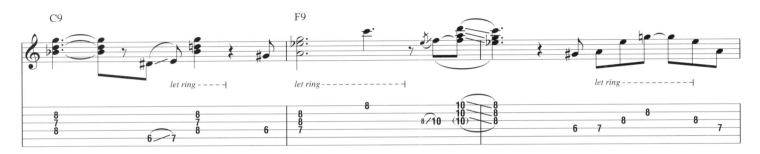

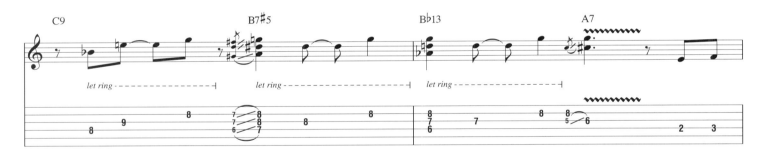

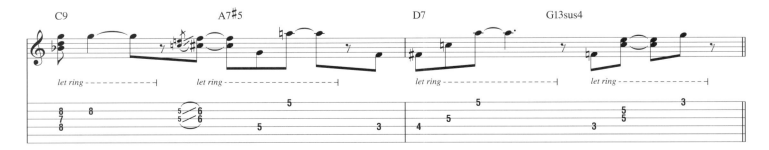

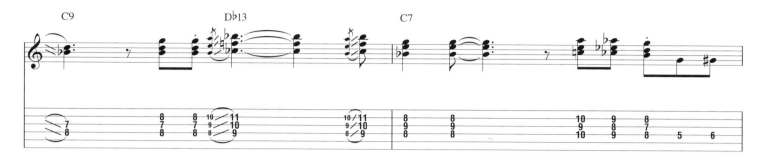

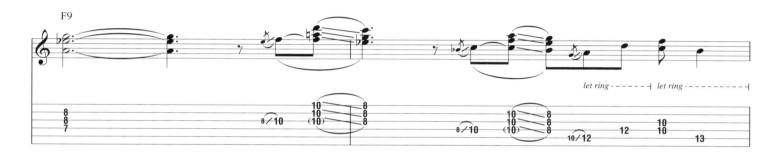

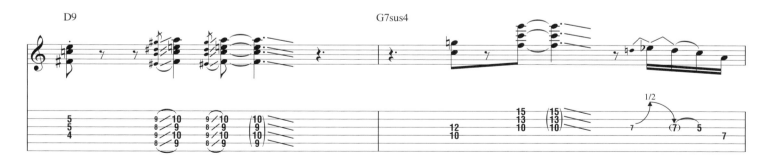

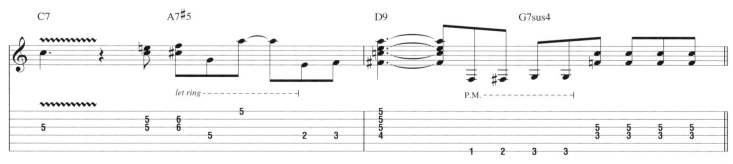

A BUZZ IN THE BOOGIE
(Key of G minor)

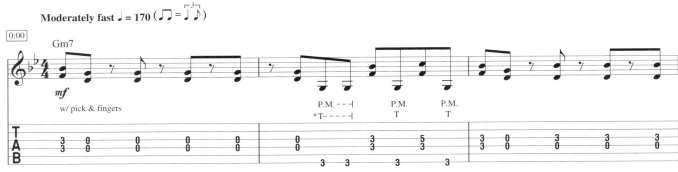

Moderately fast ♩ = 170

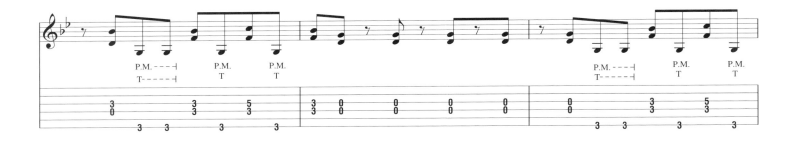

*T = Thumb on 6th string

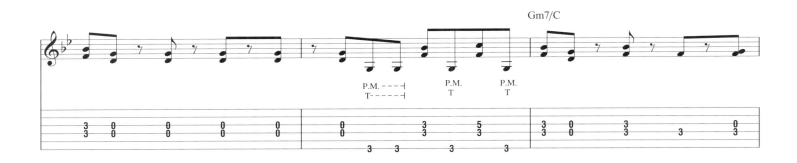

Gm7/C

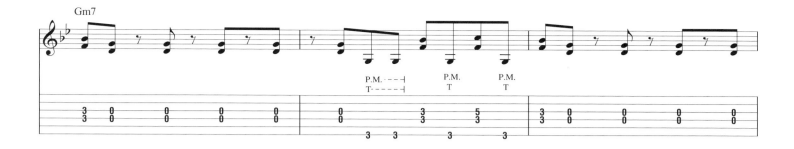

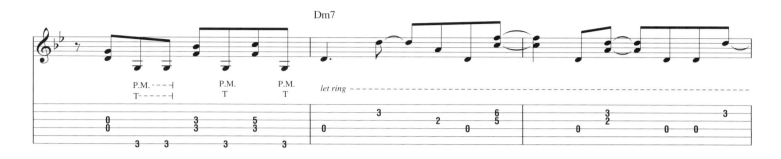

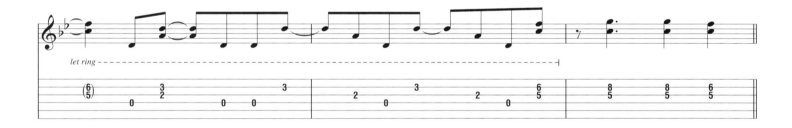

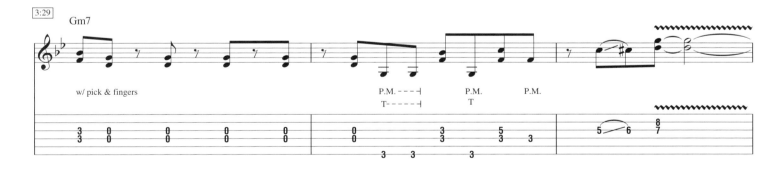

C7(no3rd)

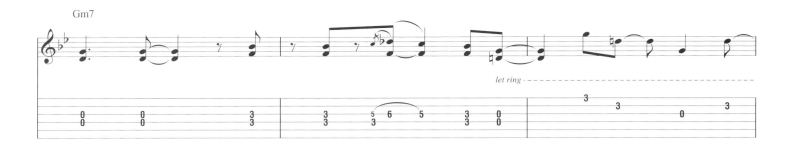

Gm7

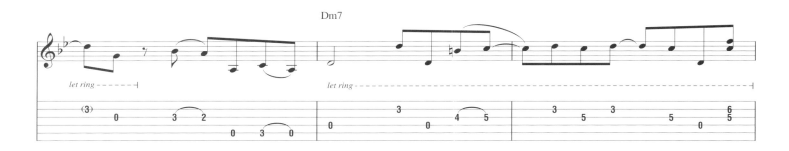

Dm7

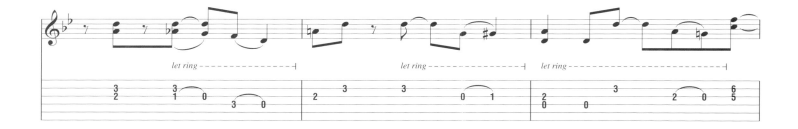

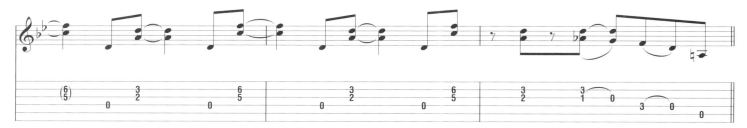

Gm7

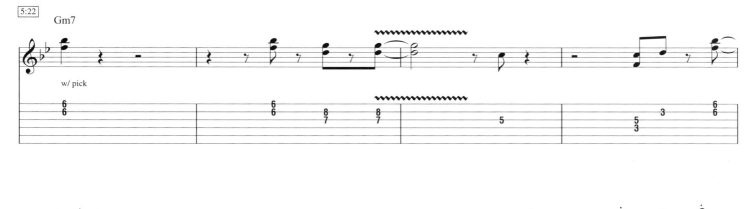

w/ pick

THE 17 JAM
(Key of C minor)

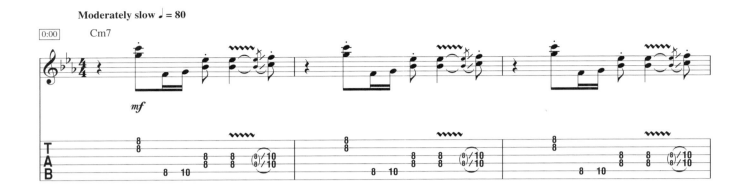

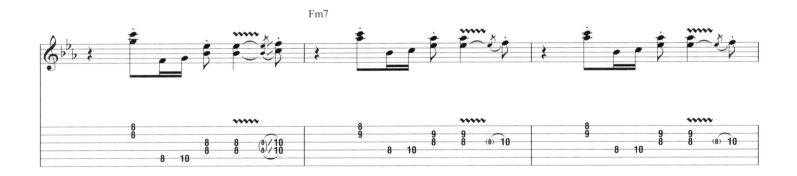

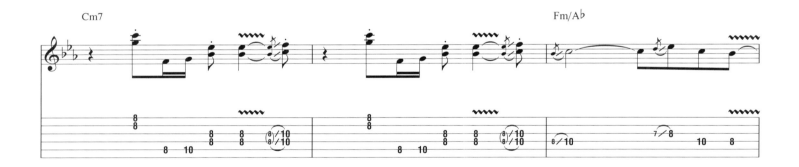

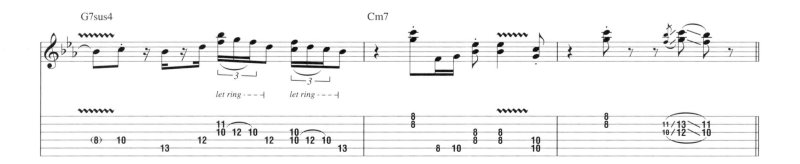

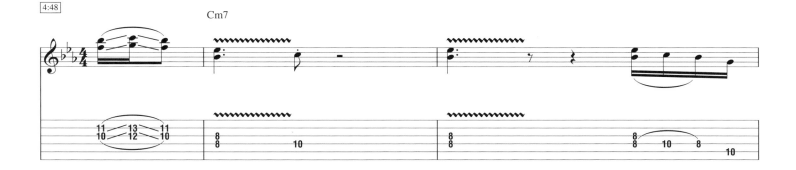

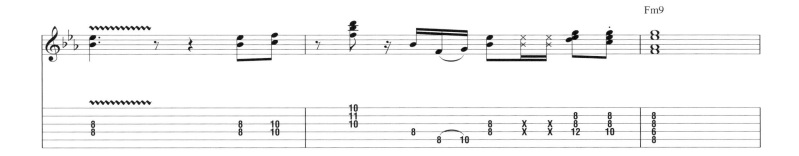

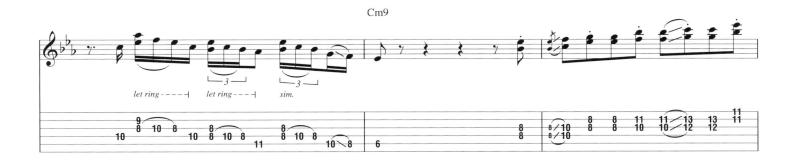

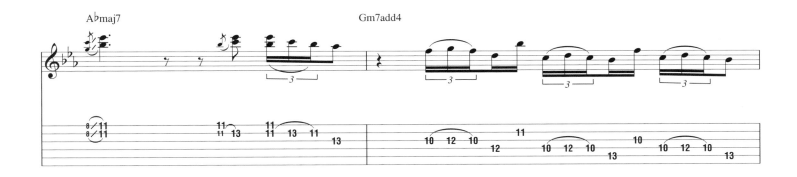

11

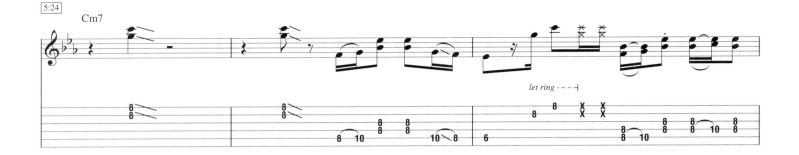

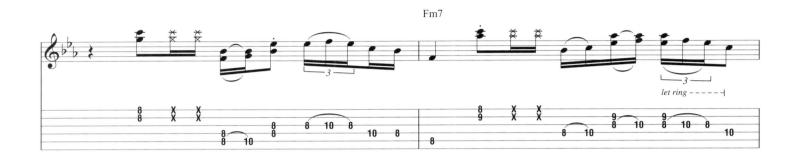

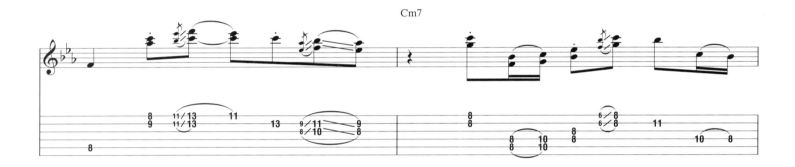

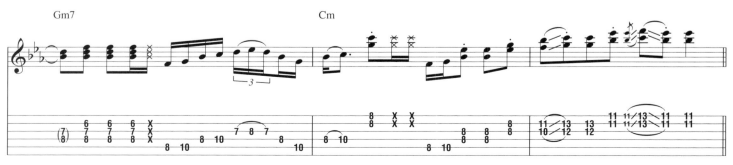

GREEN GROUND
(Key of E minor)

Moderately ♩ = 124

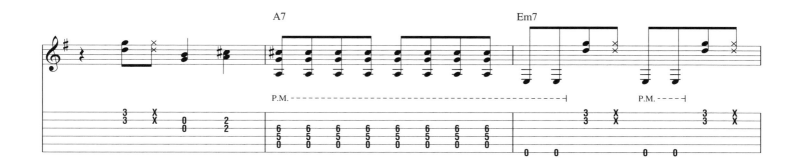

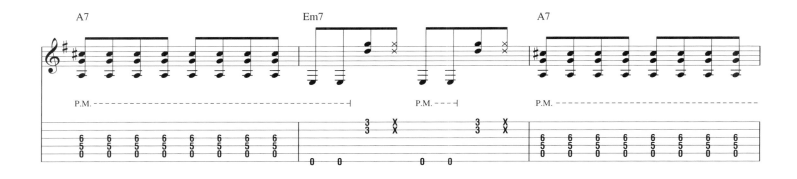

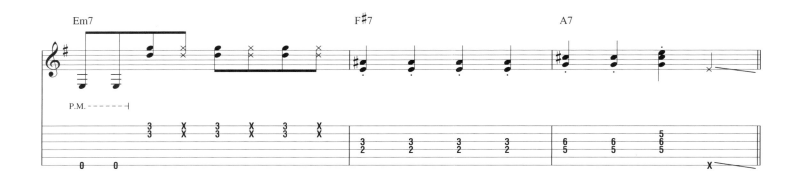

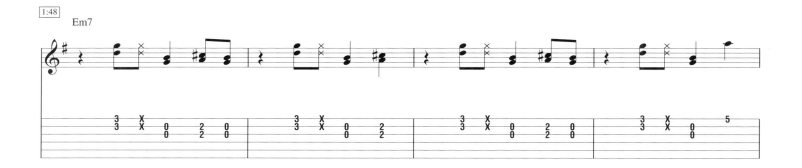

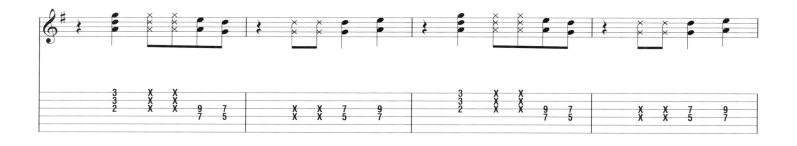

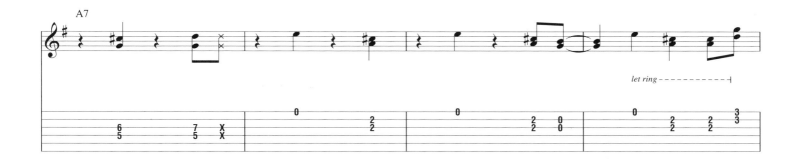

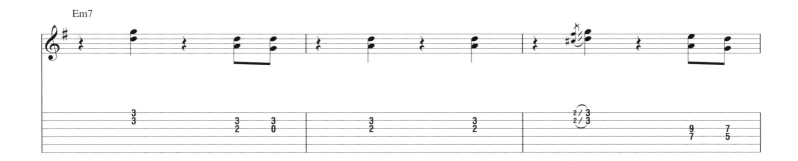

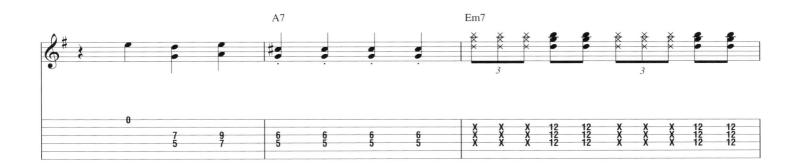

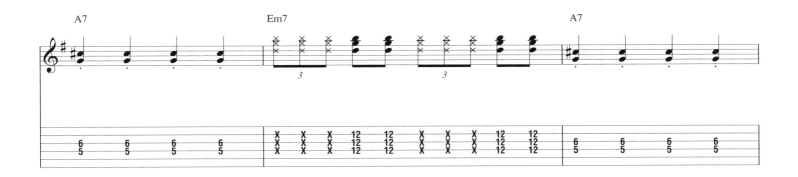

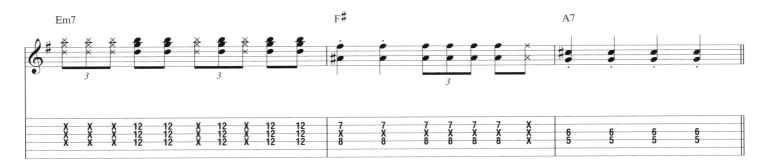

COMING TO CHICAGO
(Key of G)

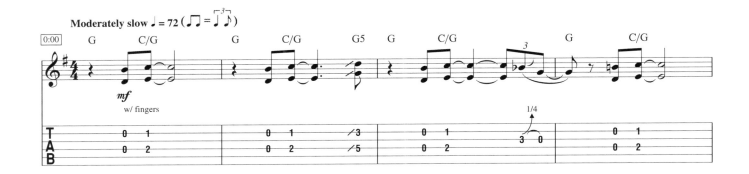

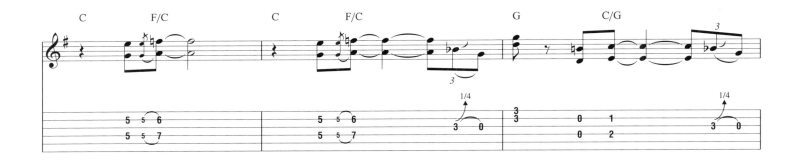

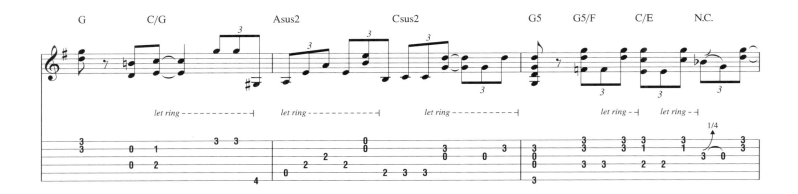

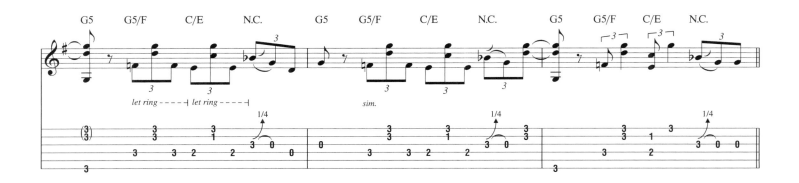

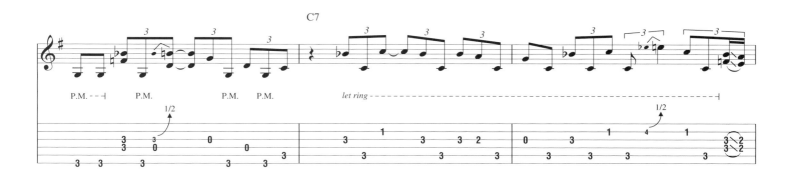

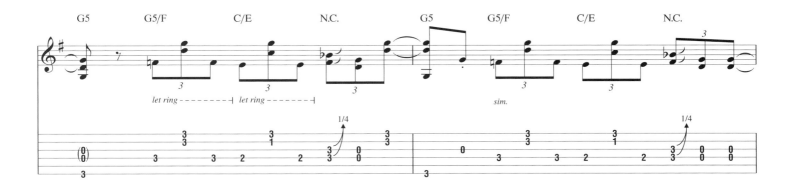

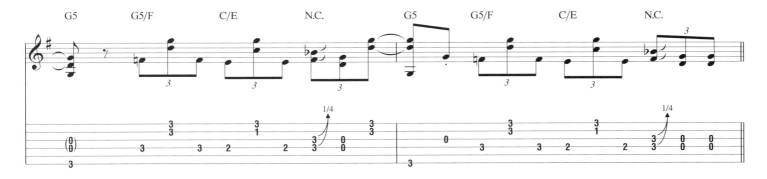

70112
(Key of D)

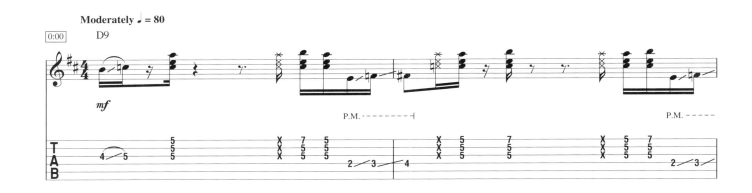

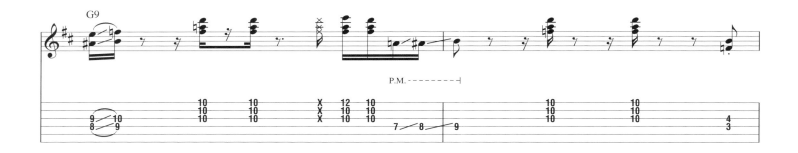

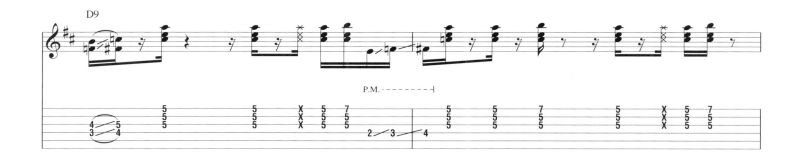

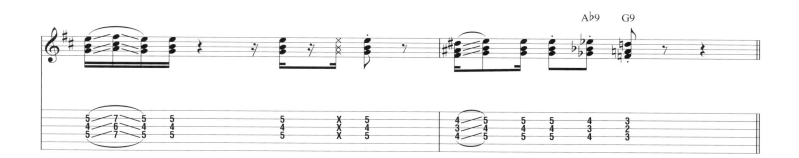

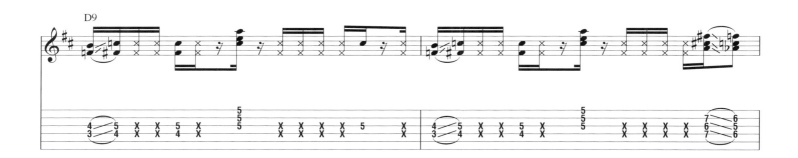

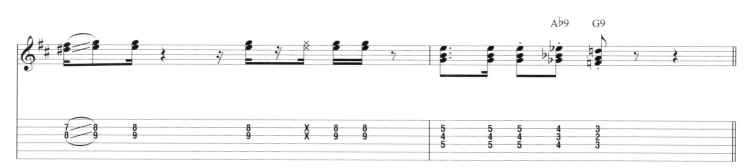

CUT THE DECK
(Key of E minor)

Moderately ♩ = 124

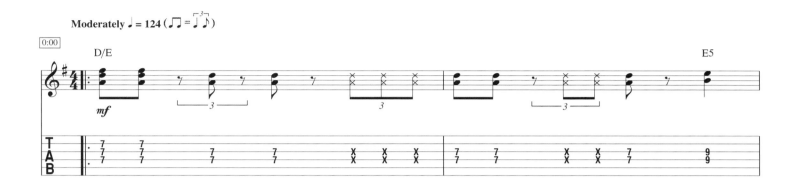

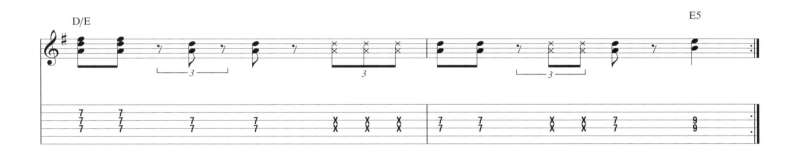

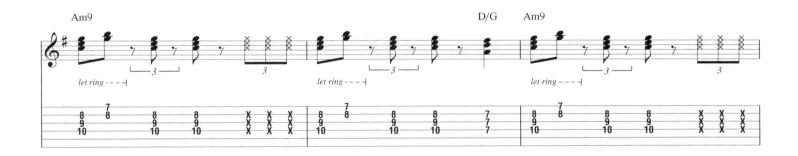

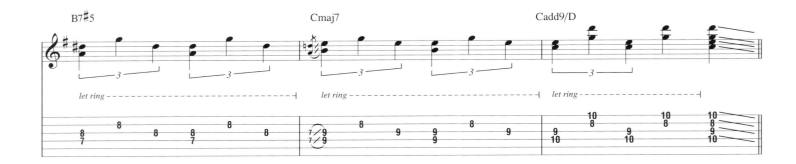

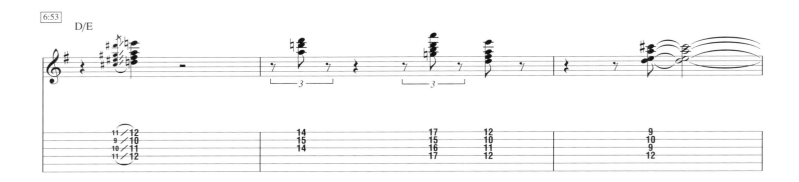

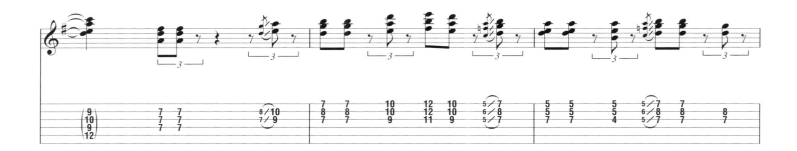

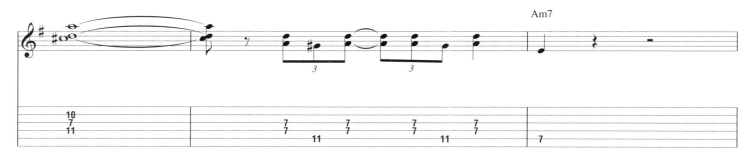

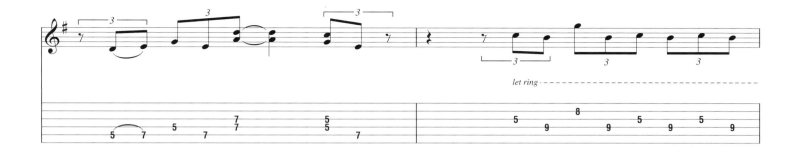

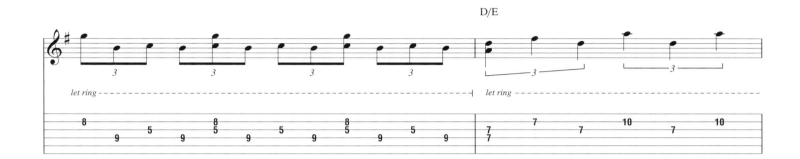

D/E

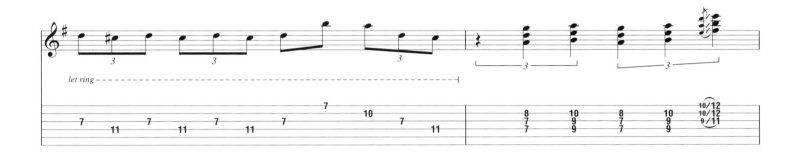

Am9   B7#5

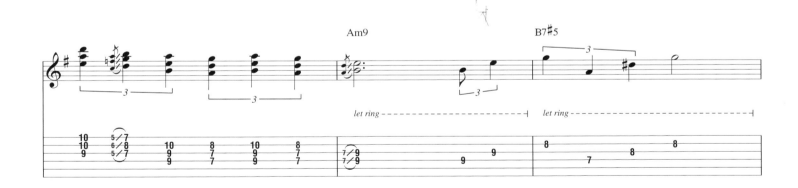

Cmaj7   Cadd9/D

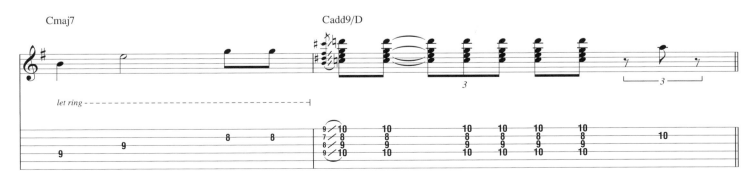